The Need For loving Attention

THE NEED FOR LOVE IN OUR LIVES

Marvin Fredman, Ph.D.

Copywrite 2008 by Marvin E. Fredman PhD.

How to Order:

Single copies may be ordered from mfredmanphd@gmail.com

Quantity discounts are also available. On your letterhead, include

information concerning the intended use of the books and the

number of books you wish to purchase.

DEDICATION

It is my honor to dedicate this book to the following people. First and foremost is my wife, Fariba, who is the most Loving person that I have ever met. Next are my children, Steffany, Marc and Samuel who have brought joy into my life and have given me the opportunity to be a Loving and involved father. My step-children, Sheila and Tina, welcomed me into their lives unselfishly and accepted my Love graciously, and to my mother who gave her unconditional Love to me. My mentor, Dr. Ralph Blanco, and his wife, Lillian, who over many years, have provided me with emotional support and guidance, that has strengthened my resolve to write about Love. In addition, I dedicate this book to all of the mental health consumers who sought out my services because they gave me the opportunity to learn, firsthand, about giving and receiving Love.

Lastly, I dedicate this book to the late Dr. Leo Buscaglia who was the remarkable man that wrote so many books about Love and who influenced my thinking so profoundly.

CONTENTS

PROLOGUE

Everybody on the planet needs Love in order to flourish. We arrive as newborn babies after having been given all of the physical supplies that were required during our intrauterine life. After birth, we require food, clothing and shelter to preserve our physical well-being. In order to preserve our psychological well-being, we need Love from our parents and others who may be on the scene. The most important people as providers of Love to newborn babies are the mother and father. Grandparents, friends and other relatives are important but only in a secondary way.

Love from the parents starts the child with a very positive experience after having left the comfort, security and warmth of the womb. Leaving the womb is known to be somewhat traumatic for the newborn.

Entering the world is a shock and so the parents Love helps the baby to make a positive adjustment to its new surroundings.

A Loving mother welcomes her child into an environment that is very different from what the womb provides. Her smile and Loving attitude has a calming effect on the baby and her Loving touch feels soothing and reassuring. The baby thrives emotionally which is exemplified by the way he or she smiles and looks contented and serene. The baby has a wonderful head start on its journey towards physical and psychological maturity.

I have been a psychologist for over thirty years. I have gained an understanding of how important Love is in the lives of women, men, teens and children. My private practice has included people as young as four to over eighty-five. A constant is that people of all ages seek Loving attention as they grow older. It is my contention that proper growth psychologically, mentally, physically and spiritually requires an ever present supply of Love from the special people that we have in our lives. I believe that we all know this fact of life even if we deny its importance.

Living on planet Earth is a golden opportunity to accomplish our goals for being alive. I want people to live productive and successful lives. I believe that we can learn about our goals and that we can learn the skills that are necessary for us to feel successful during our stay here. We have the capacity to develop ourselves into mentally alert and knowledgeable people who are aware of our inner and outer worlds.

I will be using a psycho-educational approach as an author. My plan is to present information that readers will think about and want to discuss with others. I believe that people have a natural desire to learn about themselves. I want to stimulate that desire by sharing lessons that I have learned and I hope that these lessons may have the value of improving lives in many different ways.

As a psychologist, I view myself as teacher/coach primarily. I do not think of people as patients but as curious individuals who want direction, guidance and assistance in their pursuit of positive life experiences. I am prepared to offer as much help as possible as an author. I know that it will prove beneficial and relevant.

INTRODUCTION

Did you know that every person has an inner world in addition to their outer world? Let's start with the easier one to define first. The outer world or what we can call the external world is made up of people, places and things that form the environment in which we live. All of our relationships, all of the objects that we treasure such as our houses, cars, toys, athletic equipment and pieces of art belong in the world outside of ourselves. On the other hand, all of our thoughts, feelings, desires, dreams, fears, hopes and memories belong in the world inside of ourselves. We are taught early in life by our parents to pay more attention to the outer world than to the inner world. The reason is that our parents were taught the very same lesson by their parents. The philosophy is for parents to teach their children how to fit or not to fit into society, to live up to or not to live up to the expectations of others, to value or not to value achievement and success, to please others or not to

8

please others to get what we want and, most important of all, to wear or not to wear masks that fool others into believing that we are what they believe us to be. These teachings pass from generation to generation and are considered truths that control our lives. We are programmed from early on to value or not to value the opinions of others towards ourselves and to seek or not to seek approval from relatives, friends and the other significant people in our lives. Once we are programmed in this way, we will always have a belief system that favors attending to the outer world rather than the inner one.

What are the consequences for being trained by parents and others to be unaware of the inner world? What price do we pay for such an orientation to life? The answer, very simply, is that our growth as psychological and spiritual beings becomes significantly hindered or stopped altogether. After many years of observing people dealing with their lives in my role of being a practicing psychologist I have reached a major conclusion. It is that of all of the negative things that can happen to human beings, I believe that having our growth blocked or stopped is the *WORST.*

9

I know that many readers will completely disagree with my conclusion. We can all imagine very terrible life experiences that can occur. Being raped, becoming paralyzed, losing our wealth, losing our minds and a death of a loved one are examples of tragedies that people experience. Why is having our growth blocked or stopped worse? The reason is that we are here, living on planet Earth, because we have the same mission to complete. That mission, to grow into psychologically and spiritually fit beings, is so important that failing to complete it renders our lives unsatisfactory no matter how much money that we have accumulated, how much praise that we have received for our accomplishments, how much pleasure that we have experienced from our relationships or how many children that we have had and raised. Doing all of these things is part of the human experience and belongs to outer world life. Conversely, the most important inner world issue is growing psychologically and spiritually throughout our lifetime.

I am writing this book because of my conviction in and my dedication to the growth process. I am inviting readers to join with me to learn about psychological and spiritual growth so that we, together, can represent a process that is so positive in nature. There is enough negativity in the world. We all know that! Let us commit ourselves to being agents of change that work for goodness and positive energy while we live. We can make a difference for not only ourselves but for our children and their children and for future generations. I hope that this book increases positive connections between people and that it helps readers to become providers of emotional support and love to others.

The following chapters will describe the growth process as I know it to be and how the process becomes hindered or even stopped for some people. I will discuss remedies and provide case histories of how we can remove the blockages to the growth process and strengthen it during life. I want everyone who has an interest in being able to use their inborn gifts and talents to the fullest extent possible to do so and to function maximally as parents, friends, helpers and positive contributors to the planet.

THE INNER WORLD

The inner world is a mysterious place for most people. My many years of helping people to explore the inner world has taught me that people, in general, are frightened to take a look. My clients come to me because they are experiencing distress in many different forms. They want relief as soon as possible. They do not know what is causing the distress whether it is described as anxiety, panic attacks, depression, fears, and conflict with relatives and friends, feelings of worthlessness, etc. People are used to taking medicines when they feel badly physically and usually the physical discomfort goes away quickly. The people who I see know that there are medications that are prescribed by physicians for relief of symptoms such as depression and anxiety but they are aware of the fact that being a psychologist I am unable to prescribe medication. They prefer to avoid these medications if at all possible. We live in a society that wants "a quick fix." I have to explain to my clients that I do not believe in quick fixes but, instead, hard work which takes more time. I have learned that symptoms of distress will disappear if the correct psychological work is done. Some of the people that hear this do not come back. Some do!

A beautifully written account of the inner world was given to me a long time ago. It was written by Charles C. Finn in September 1966, who was able to present an emotionally appealing request for help with an inner world issue. The title is *"Please Hear What I Am Not Saying."*

"Don't be fooled by me. Don't be fooled by the face I wear. For I wear a mask, I wear a thousand masks. Masks that I'm afraid to take off. And none of them are me. Pretending is an art that's second nature with me. But don't be fooled, for God's sake don't be fooled. I give you the impression that I'm secure. That all is sunny and unruffled with me, within as well as without, that confidence is my name and coolness my game, but don't believe me. Please.

My surface may seem smooth, but my surface is my mask, my ever-varying and ever-concealing mask. Beneath lies no smugness; no complacence. Beneath dwells the real me in confusion, in fear, in aloneness, but I hide this. I don't want anybody to know it. I panic at the thought of my weakness and fear of being exposed. That's why I frantically create a mask to hide behind. A nonchalant, sophisticated façade, to help me pretend, to shield me from the glance that knows.

But such a glance is precisely my salvation. My only salvation. And I know it. That is if it's followed by acceptance, if it's followed by love. It's the only thing that can liberate me, from myself, from my own self-built prison walls, from the barriers that I so painstakingly erect. It's the only thing that will assure me of what I can't assure myself that I'm really worth something. But I don't tell you this. I don't dare. I'm afraid to. I'm afraid you'll think less of me, that you'll laugh, and your laugh would kill me. I'm afraid that you will see this and reject me.

So I play my game, my desperate pretending game, with a façade of assurance without, and a trembling child within. The glittering but empty parade of masks. And my life becomes a front. I idly chatter to you in the suave tones of surface talk. I tell you everything that's really nothing, and nothing of what's everything, of what's crying within me. So when I'm going through my routine do not be fooled by what I'm saying.

Please listen carefully and try to hear what I'm saying, what I'd like to be able to say, what for survival I need to say, but what I can't say I dislike hiding. Honestly, I dislike the superficial game. I'd really like to be genuine and spontaneous, and me, but you've got to help me. You've got to hold out your hand even when that's the last thing I seem to want or need. Only you can wipe away from my eyes the blank stare of the breathing dead.

Only you can call me into aliveness. Each time you're kind, and gentle, and encouraging, each time you try to understand because you really care, my heart begins to grow wings, very small wings, very feeble wings but wings. With your sensitivity and sympathy, and your power of understanding, you can breathe life into me. I want you to know that. I want you to know how important you are to me, how you can be a creator of the person that is me if you choose to, please choose to. You alone can break down the wall behind which I tremble. You alone can remove my mask. You alone can release me from my shadow world of panic and uncertainty, from my lonely prison.

So please do not pass me by. Please do not pass me by. It will not be easy for you. A long conviction of worthlessness builds strong walls. The nearer you approach to me, the blinder I may strike back. It's irrational but despite what books say about man, I am irrational. I fight against the very thing I cry out for. But I am told that love is stronger than walls, and in this lies my hope, my only hope. Please try to beat down those walls with firm hands, but with gentle hands–for the child is very sensitive.

Who am I, you may wonder, I am someone you know very well. For I am every man you meet, I am every woman you meet and I am every child you meet."

• • •

Helping people to look inside themselves and to work on their core issues is challenging to anyone who volunteers to do it. Early in my career as a psychologist I became aware of my mission. It was to become the kind of person who could be trusted by others to be invited into their inner worlds so that inner healing could take place. I will call this inner healing "recovery work" so it is not confused with the physical healing process of humans. What I mean is that people are born with the ability to recover from major psychological traumas provided that they get the help that is required. Being a helper to traumatized people means that the helper must be prepared to be very patient, very understanding, very committed and very supportive emotionally. Also, the helper has to have the specialized skills that are necessary. Years of specialized experience and training provide the helper with not only knowledge of the recovery process but a familiarity of the different interventions that must be used.

I had an opportunity to help a severely traumatized woman whom I will name Belle that I met in 1978. Since Belle, I have worked with many other emotionally traumatized men and women but she remains what seems like a miraculous example of how people can recover and heal themselves from devastating psychological injury. Watching her go through a process of emotional recovery that took many, many years convinced me that we ALL have the ability to heal ourselves if we are provided with the necessary supplies by people who love us and who are committed to the recovery process. My admiration for Belle grew as she transformed herself from a highly depressed young woman who could barely function in the world to a happily married and productive employee who is held in high regard by her employer. Here is her story.

Belle

I met Belle when she was seventeen years old. She came to see me because she was severely depressed. She stated that she felt more like forty years old than a teenager because of everything that she had been through. Belle said that she had crammed so much into her seventeen years that she had to grow up quickly into a woman even though she was still a young person. She was convinced that she would die before turning thirty-five. I have her permission to tell her story in the hope that others will feel encouraged to do what is necessary for self-restoration.

One of the most psychologically damaging experiences a child can have is to be the victim of sexual abuse by a parent or sibling. In Belle's life, it was done by her older half-brother whom I will call James. James was thirteen when he first initiated the sexual abuse process of his sister. She was only five when her brother began to play with her in "a new way". He became more physical and began touching her more and more. At first, it was merely tickling and wrestling around in what seemed an innocent time of fun for a brother and sister. Belle loved James and looked forward to spending time with him. What she did not know, of course, was that her brother had more than play on his mind. He was engaged in a sinister and evil plot to ruin his sister's life. Why? We don't know. Perhaps he hated Belle because she was the "baby" of the family which took attention away from him. It is not uncommon for an older sibling to feel anger towards a younger sibling and want that child harmed. In any case, his behavior was not motivated by loving feelings for Belle or just the need to express his sexual urges. That would have been destructive enough to his sister.

This teen's destructive tendencies showed themselves in the malicious and hateful way that he treated Belle. Not only did James rape her during her fifth year of life but he continued sexually abusing her for seven more years. By the time he was finished, James had punched Belle numerous times, threatened to kill her repeatedly and treated her like she was a worthless and disgusting piece of trash.

Belle endured the physical and psychological pain at the hands of her brother without telling anyone about it. She was too frightened of James and too ashamed of herself to stop it or to ask for help from anyone. So it went on and on doing more psychological damage to her. By the time that I met Belle she trusted no man, viewed herself as a sexual object to be used by men, prostituted herself for drugs and material possessions and truly hated herself.

Belle's history included being born into a family with an alcoholic father and a psychologically dysfunctional mother. It was obvious to Belle as she was growing up that her mother preferred James who was from a previous marriage. Belle's mother treated her daughter coldly and without much affection. On the other hand, James could do no wrong in his mother's eyes.

Belle's father was very loving towards Belle which promoted more of a close feeling between him and his daughter than between Belle and her mother. He was a very sensitive man who was a professional artist. When sober, he was attentive to Belle's emotional needs and was emotionally supportive to his daughter. Not unexpectedly, there was constant friction between Belle's parents which led to a divorce when Belle was nine years old. Belle's mother hated her ex-husband and she tried to ruin Belle's relationship with her father any way that she could. Belle's father became more and more alienated from Belle over time. Belle's love for her father was powerful and sustaining even though she did not see him for long periods of time. Eventually, Belle's father died of alcoholism.

Belle's mother was an emotionally immature woman who was unable to provide Belle with a stable home life. She was, no doubt, a depressed person which was a natural consequence of being married to a severe alcoholic who clashed with her constantly. During her marriage to Belle's father she was, for all intents and purposes, a single mother who felt overwhelmed, unloved, emotionally unsupported and burdened with a nuisance of a daughter.

Belle grew up feeling violated, vulnerable, unprotected and unsafe within her own home. Her father moved out before the divorce and Belle lost contact with him as her mother prevented his visitation. Cut off physically and emotionally from her father and victimized by her brother, she was unable to develop positive peer relationships in school and in the neighborhood. Belle kept to herself, sad and miserable.

A child such as this obviously fails to thrive emotionally and spiritually. Her personal growth is stunted so that she remains fixated at an age far younger than her chronological age. Her needs are those of a very young child, even infantile--immediate gratification, security and safety, belonging to someone who cares and gives genuine affection. Such a young person is impulsive, ready to grab and clutch possessively at objects, sensations and people who seem to satisfy her powerful yet normal needs. Very predictably, as a teenager Belle turned to alcohol and drugs, became promiscuous with both men and women and selected emotionally immature partners who were punishing, abandoning, rejecting and abusive. She got herself into situations in which she was further raped. To add to Belle's ever increasing sense of shame and worthlessness, she had abortions which were contrary to her religious beliefs. Each encounter left her feeling more negative about herself and her "friends," contributing to the serious depression she was experiencing when we first met.

Belle presented as a highly attractive seventeen-year-old with long brown hair. On the surface, Belle tried to look physically fit, fresh, positive and energetic and a person ready to enjoy life to the maximum. However, the Belle I saw was hidden from others. She was deeply depressed, suicidal and barely able to sit up in my office. Belle was so "burned out" by life that she slouched on the sofa with her head back, looking like her life force had drained away. She believed that there was no point in continuing to live. Belle promised me that she would not take her own life as long as I had hope for her in the future. When asked if she wanted me to help her, she responded with "Yes, but I don't think that it'll do any good." In spite of her dark pessimism, we agreed to meet twice weekly.

I learned, long before I had met Belle that people who seek psychological assistance are emotionally wounded and desire to recover from the injuries that were inflicted upon them by others. Such people are looking for someone who is going to love them even though this desire is usually unknown to them. They come in wanting answers to questions about what is wrong with them. What they really want is loving attention but typically are afraid to ask for it or to recognize their need. There is usually a crisis involved which has caused feelings of anxiety or depression. It is the rare individual who is aware of needing help because of deep but hidden emotional pain and "core" issues.

I was able to see Belle's suffering at the very beginning of our relationship. I offered her my assistance which meant that, having experienced such severe abuse, Belle would need years of my kindness, understanding, compassion and encouragement. I will call this attention from me Unconditional Love (Love). I will be discussing Love from what is commonly called love in a later chapter.

I promised Belle that I would not abandon her emotionally and that I would try my hardest to be accepting of her as we worked together. Understandably, Belle did not believe that I would volunteer to offer such consistent emotional support and she was doubtful of my commitment to her. It took Belle many years to believe that I meant what I had stated. For a long time, she anticipated that I would grow weary of her endless negative moods, thoughts and feelings and just "dump" her. Seven years later Belle told me that she trusted me finally not to give up on her and to continue to be a Loving person in her life.

Belle and I spent many hours together in my office with me listening as she was able to reveal her life experiences. Over time, Belle was able to "peel back the layers of the onion" so to speak and expose gradually the horrors underneath. She shared with me that she was brutally self-abusive and would whip her back and verbally condemn herself. Her need for punishment to "make up" for her self-believed evil behavior continued for a long time. Belle was so angry with so many people that she experienced rages and crying spells frequently. It was during these periods of intense anger that Belle would accuse me of abandoning her, becoming disinterested in her feelings, faking my concerns, planning to get rid of her and merely listening "just because it's your job." My reaction was to continue showing Love by being tolerant, compassionate and reassuring.

Belle had learned to hate herself because she was taught by her mother to feel guilty whenever she did not live up to her mother's code of moral conduct. By the time that I met Belle, she had committed numerous "sins" and thus had labeled herself a "sinner" who deserved physical and emotional punishment to be administered by herself and others. Eventually, through self-examination, inner building of positive self-beliefs, group exercises so that she could express her negative feelings and receive emotional support from group mates and my continued help, Belle became able to be Loving towards herself, acknowledge her positive qualities and involve herself in relationships which were not psychologically injurious to her.

In group settings supervised by me Belle had many opportunities to confront her sexually abusive brother in role-playing situations. Role-playing allows a group member to confront an abuser by using a group mate as a stand-in. These confrontations, though very often intense emotionally, are a necessary part of the self-healing process. Belle spewed out her hatred of him and was able to yell and scream about what he did to her. Belle confronted many other people from the past with her negative feelings. People who had raped and beat her, disappointed and mistreated her or violated her trust. She worked hard to become self-forgiving and forgiving of others, even including her brother.

Belle learned to be very wary of any man who wanted access to her inner world. In the past, Belle was attracted to men that she thought of as "low life scum bags" and "sleazy." Her experiences with her brother taught Belle different lessons about men. One was that men who professed love for her are dangerous and not to be trusted. Another was that men were not motivated by Love but by their desires for physical and emotional gratification. A third was that she was an object to be used by men who were psychologically immature and who wanted their egos stroked. Belle became convinced that she was unable to have a satisfactory relationship with a man and so she turned to women instead. Belle was bi-sexual for many years and she believed that homosexuality was to be her final, safe choice.

Belle is an example of how the human spirit can live on even when a person experiences severe psychological trauma. She never settled for a ruined life but kept working on herself year after year. I am pleased to report that Belle is married happily to the "Love of her life." He is a man who is very compatible with her, Loves her and that they are real partners in life. She and I will continue to have contact with each other non-professionally as long as she desires.

THE PATH

I have good news and I have bad news for all readers. The good news is that for each and every person there is a path upon which to travel that will bring true happiness, prosperity and fulfillment. The bad news is that very few people know about the path and, consequently, are traveling upon it. The path that I am referring to is the path that represents a mixture of ongoing psychological and spiritual growth that can be experienced up until we take our last breath of life. Ideally, every person is taught about the growth path so that it would be possible to monitor how he or she is progressing on the path we would be able to answer the following questions: Am I on my path? Have I deviated from the path? Am I not on the path but instead traveling in time as a lost individual but do not know it? It would seem to me that the path that I am describing is either unknown to most people or not fully understood. We are not taught about it in depth while we are students in school even through college or beyond. Maybe we have been introduced to psychological processes to a minimal degree by reading a book or having taken a class on the subject. There is so much more to learn about ourselves as psychological beings than can be explained in a book or in a class about psychology in high school or college. With regards to spiritual growth, there are many people that have learned relevant concepts because of an affiliation with one religion or another and the teachings that have been presented. I am not here to discuss the merits of religious practices but, instead, to share what I have learned about the nature of spiritual growth and I hope that I do not offend anyone who has different ideas than my own.

The concept that I embrace is that the process of spiritual growth leads to our becoming truly Loving people. The goal of spiritual growth is for us to evolve into individuals who, at times, can be kind, compassionate and emotionally supportive. I believe that there are very few people on the planet that can be like this all of the time. For the rest of us, it is a matter of how much of our waking life are we able to be Loving towards others. I will define love in the next chapter but for now I mean the ability to provide positive energy to another individual.

Psychological growth, on the other hand, has nothing to do with Love. Love involves the spiritual domain and not the psychological domain. Psychological growth pertains to the psyche which can be defined as that part of ourselves which is not of the body but of the mind and emotions. Psychological growth has to do with evolving from emotionally immature persons to emotionally mature ones. Before going into detail about the evolution of emotional maturity I want to provide an overview of how we function in a more total context.

Human beings have four different selves that exist simultaneously. We can refer to them as four different realities of consciousness. They are the physical consciousness, the emotional consciousness, the mental consciousness and the spiritual consciousness. Only one of them can be experienced at any given time. We are in the physical reality when we are aware of a physical sensation like a pain in the arm, an itch, a feeling of bodily pleasure or a hunger pang. At that moment, our physical body is our one and only focus and the other three realities are excluded from our consciousness. The emotional self is experienced when we have an emotional reaction to anything such as a person, a situation or something that we hear or see. When we have any kind of a feeling like joy, sadness, anger or fear it is not possible to be aware of our thoughts because the mental reality has been turned off. We would have to switch out of the emotional consciousness to the mental consciousness in order to explain to someone what we are reacting to emotionally. How many times do we ask an angry person "What are you angry about?" expecting the person to feel anger and think about the reasons at the same time. It cannot be done. Instead, ask the person to express the feelings and wait for the anger to subside before trying to understand the reasons for the anger, pain, etc.

The third reality, the mental consciousness, has taken over when we are trying to compute the answer to a math problem, contemplating the future or worrying about how to pay a bill. The fact that the active consciousness is mental means that we are unable to have an emotional feeling at the same time until we leave the mental self and switch to the emotional self. It is pointless to ask someone to respond emotionally to a situation or a person when the other individual is busy thinking. *For example, it frustrates many wives when they are feeling frightened about one of their children's behavior problems in school and they want their husband to react emotionally even though he is trying to figure out the household budget. She mistakenly believes that he could care less because he was unable to feel the same way at the moment. She needed to give him time to shift from the mental self to the emotional self.*

Lastly, we are in the spiritual self when we are in a Loving place. We must access our spiritual reality if we want to feel compassion or a feeling of humanitarianism. Otherwise, it would be impossible to reach out to someone Lovingly. There is a difference between attending to someone out of duty or a feeling of responsibility and offering love to someone who needs it. Offering advice can be helpful or not helpful for any one person at any given time but offering Love IS always helpful anytime. The problem is that many of us have difficulty accessing the spiritual reality because we are so used to being in one of the other three realities the rest of the time. By this I mean that we can become too physically minded, too emotional or too mental.

One common example is people that spend so much of their time attending to their bodies because of vanity or a preoccupation with their appearance. Their need to be adored and to be admired by others is so important that they commit a considerable amount of energy into creating a body that impresses others with its beauty, musculature, physical dimensions or skin tone. Being so focused upon the physical body makes it difficult to be balanced among all of the realities. My recommendation is that all people need to explore all four areas of consciousness so that one or more will not be excluded from experiencing life.

Finding and staying on the path requires that we know and accept ourselves thoroughly. We are born with tendencies that are with us during our lifetime. There are many, many tendencies or predispositions to consider which makes the job of really knowing ourselves a difficult one. The main reason is that certain tendencies are easier for us to accept while others cause us to feel emotionally uncomfortable. Our natural inclination is to AVOID dealing with aspects of ourselves that result in feeling anxious or ashamed. To feel emotionally comfortable, we focus attention on the aspects that we like best. Conversely, we ignore or deny that there are tendencies that are socially unacceptable such as being an independent thinker who speaks his or her mind, a person who shares deep feelings which are often kept private such as depression, inadequacy, inferiority or fearfulness, a person who shows affection in public, a person who would rather be alone than to be with people just to be socially popular or a person who has the courage to not exploit others for selfish reasons. We are taught by a variety of people what is or is not socially acceptable. Crying in public for men is typically frowned upon for males that are no longer babies. These teachings are internalized and are locked in our mind forever. We cannot get rid of them because they are permanently stored in memory unless the memory portion of our brain is destroyed. The only option is for us to learn a new set of teachings that will gradually take over for the old ones. Sounds easy? It is not! It is far easier to hold onto the old teachings than to replace them. It takes years of reprogramming the mind to accomplish it.

3

THE JOURNEY

In Chapter 2 I discussed the concept that every individual has their own path to experience which will result in success in life. By success I mean a successful completion of that person's primary mission on planet Earth. It is my belief that each of us has a high priority mission to accomplish while alive. Some people are sure that they know what their mission is, others are in doubt and others have no idea. There are systems of thought that have developed over the years that try to explain to us how to know about our mission. Examples are astrology, numerology, religions and philosophies that have been put forth by many different individuals over the centuries.

It is not my goal to try to convince anyone that a particular explanation about life missions is the "right" one. Let us just say that I have come to understand what my mission is and that knowing it has helped me to make sense of my life experiences. I have always been an open-minded person and so I enjoy learning about different systems that explain the purpose of life. Of course it is often confusing when studying different systems because they often disagree with each other, present concepts that are alien or contrary to our own beliefs or require us to follow procedures that are not emotionally comfortable for us. It is too bad that we may negate or invalidate useful informational systems because of our biases or fears and so we may miss out on the potential benefits.

I am hoping to encourage readers to consider that being alive is not just a random event but that being alive carries with it the responsibility of deciding what is to be accomplished by every individual before death takes place. Knowing the mission is a cornerstone of the Journey.

The Journey begins when life begins and for our purposes ends with death. It is beyond the scope of this book to consider whether there is an afterlife that waits for us after death. Millions and millions of people believe that there is one and millions believe that there is not one. Instead, I am going to concentrate on the process of life in physical form only.

I believe that every person is a combination of spirit and physical body. The spirit part is referred to as the ethereal body. The ethereal body and the physical body are connected and remain so until death of the physical body. The journey for each person is to grow maximally as spiritual beings and as psychological beings before physical death occurs. That means that people are capable of self-improvement until we take our last breath providing the brain is still functioning in the needed way. The ultimate goal of the journey is to master being able to give and receive Love.

It is now time to discuss Love about which I have learned within my role as a practicing psychologist for many years. My learning has come from spending so much time with so many people that I tried to help. My clients have been children, adolescents and adults from ages four through eighty-six. My understanding of Love did not come from my graduate school training. Talking to so many people that needed psychological help and were willing to share their feelings openly and honestly taught me what Love is and what Love is not.

First, I want to explain that love is not Love. Love is not an emotion. It is not a feeling. Love is positive energy that can be transferred from one person to another. It is not related to the emotional self but to the spiritual self. We can say that it is experienced within the soul and not the psyche.

Every human being has the ability to react emotionally to people, places, things and thoughts. Emotions involve complex interactions within the brain. For our purposes, we will simplify the process by recognizing that we all have an emotion center in our brain called the hypothalamus that makes it possible for us to feel anger and fear. The hypothalamus is NOT INVOLVED with Love. The hypothalamus is connected to the emotional self and not the spiritual self. It is not possible to feel Love if we are reacting emotionally. We must shift out of the emotional self and into the spiritual self in order to feel Love. Therefore, we do not fall in and out of Love as writers like to say. Instead, we move from Love to love without realizing what is happening.

It is now time to discuss love which is emotionally based and not spiritually based. What we call love is a state of excitability that involves biochemical reactions taking place within the brain. There is no such thing as "falling in love." Instead, we, ourselves, create a euphoric feeling by thinking certain thoughts about the person that we now "love." It is an emotional high that we feel that comes and goes like all high feelings do. Most people are unaware of how they talk themselves into having a romantic feeling about another person. We all have a list of positive attributes that we look for in other people. If we find someone with many of these positive qualities then we become interested. The more qualities that we find in someone else then the more excited we feel. We confuse this feeling of excitement with Love and mistakenly believe that we have "fallen in love." Humans crave Love so much that love is valued whenever we think that we found it. Like taking a drug that makes us feel high, "falling in love" does the same thing. We become addicted to the high feeling because it is so stimulating. I believe that most of us feel deprived of Love as children, teens and adults that we settle for a "high" feeling whether it be a romantically based relationship, acquiring wealth and/

or power, winning at a poker game or anything else that "turns us on."

My belief system is that we are in human form because we need to learn how to give and receive Love. Being able to give and to receive Love is a spiritually based matter. It is not an emotionally based matter. It has nothing to do with feeling excited, stimulated or high. In a sense, we have been taught by society to become emotional "junkies." We have been taught by authors of romanticism that we should seek out someone that possesses the qualities that we admire so much. For example, a woman values a man who is sensitive, Loving, considerate, kind, comforting, attentive, reliable, dependable, thoughtful and sincere. If she encounters a man who appears to have these qualities then she begins to feel an attraction to him. Immediately, she places a high value upon him and wants him for herself. She will then do whatever she can to make herself valued by that man because she believes that he is the "right" man for her. She becomes convinced of her choice because she has "fallen in love" with him which justifies, in her mind, that they should be together. The woman is allowing her emotional self to rule over her decisions about her life.

41

The emotional self accounts for our feelings, but not our ability to think rationally and logically. We need our mental self for that. What if the man that she has met has learned how to present himself to women as though he possesses the qualities that she admires?

How does she know that he is for real and not just showing her the many masks that he wears?

Perhaps, he has learned about females as he was growing up and now knows what they tend to value in males. He craves female attention and so he presents himself as the "right" man and is willing to continue the courtship because he gets what he desires.

My recommendation is for males and females to become knowledgeable about Love and love so that we are mindful about the inner workings of relationships. Maybe, our selection process would be more effective in choosing the "right" person and we would find that the divorce rate goes down and there is less emotional trauma experienced by so many people in their interpersonal relationships. What I have found is that the majority of people in our society prefer to continue the pattern of wanting to "fall in love" rather than giving it up. I have had many clients lose their interest in working on their growth when I suggested that "falling in love"is an addiction and needs to be avoided.

4

BEGINNINGS

We are all experiencing our own journey as we live our life. Hopefully, we are on the path that will result in our psychological and spiritual growth. We come into life with traits that will be with us throughout our lifetime. Certainly, the environment impacts us significantly but much of who we are as human beings is built into the person. There is still a great deal of controversy among mental health professionals about the influence of the environment as it affects the development of a child's personality versus the notion that personality characteristics are inborn.

I admit that many years ago I was confused about these issues. Today, I am less confused. After many years of helping people with psychological problems, I have decided that we arrive with strengths and weaknesses, predispositions of many kinds, a set of values that we adhere to and an agenda of challenges that we are to face and overcome if at all possible. What we become as individuals has to do with who we are at birth and what happens to us on our journey.

It may be hard for many people to believe that personality characteristics are present at birth. Here are some examples of inborn traits. How sensitive a person is to his or her environment is built in. How selfish a person is, how controlling a person is, how Loving a person is, how creative a person is and how aggressive a person is are built in. I could list hundreds more but I think I've made my point. What I am describing goes beyond genetics. I think that these characteristics are present as part of our journey and not because our parents passed them on to us. We have these traits which may or may not make us like our parents because a Higher Power made sure that we have what we need for the journey that we are taking. The strengths help us to succeed and the weaknesses require us to work even harder to succeed.

I believe that the weaknesses, the handicaps, the predispositions and the defects that we may have are there not as curses but opportunities to show our dedication to the growth process. It is easy to blame our lack of success on our journey on to areas of weakness or on handicaps rather than on our own inability to rise to the occasion. The kind of growth that I am referring to requires that a person work very hard throughout one's lifetime. How do environmental influences aid us to have a successful journey or almost guarantee that we will not?

We are subjected to environmental influences as soon as we are born. The birth mother is there to welcome us to planet Earth. It is very important that the baby is welcomed and not rejected by the mother. If rejected, the baby becomes scarred for life. Psychological trauma occurs. That child will spend the rest of his or her life believing that he or she is unlovable, that he or she is meant to suffer emotionally, that he or she is doomed to a life of rejection and discontentedness and he or she is condemned to always long for a mother's love but never receive it. Maternal rejection of the baby seriously harms the infant.

On the other hand, if the birth mother is Loving and welcoming then the baby will respond positively to the environment. We will see a contented baby. We will see a baby that is alert, aware of its surroundings, responsive to care-givers and able to give and receive Love.

Why do mothers reject their babies when they are born? Some mothers are depressed, some mothers have personalities that make it impossible for them to be Loving, some mothers are anxious and insecure which cause them to be withdrawn and distant and some mothers do not have much of a maternal instinct. Not all women who have the ability to birth a child are equipped to Love that child. We take for granted that mothers are able to Love their children. NOT TRUE! Even separation from the mother because of medical reasons which certainly negatively affects the baby can be minimized by a Loving mother. Babies who are Loved thrive. Babies who are not Loved barely survive emotionally even if they survive physically.

What about fathers? A father's Love is very important to the well-being of the baby. It is second in importance to a mother's Love but it is still essential. A baby comes equipped with the ability to bond with both of his parents. Bonding with only the mother will have a negative effect on the child's psychological growth during its lifetime. Sometimes, the father is unavailable not because he does not want to be but due to unavoidable reasons. What is important is that people tend to downplay the value of fatherly Love which is a big mistake. We need to teach men that they are really needed by their children to provide the emotional support that only a father figure can give. Love from a father teaches the child that men can be trusted, that men value their children and that men can be depended upon to satisfy the child's needs for security, affection, positive attention and validation that the child is wanted and lovable.

A father's rejection teaches children different things, such as men are self-centered and immature creatures, that men are selfish and only concern themselves with their own self interest and that men are incapable of being Loving and devoted parents. Learning these lessons stay in the child's mind throughout its lifetime and have a profound effect on both the son and the daughter. Since all children have a built-in need to imitate their parents, the parents serve as models which are stored permanently in the child's mind. The son is destined to be like his father with regard to his attitudes, values and beliefs. A rejecting father teaches his son to be self-rejecting as well as becoming a selfish and self-absorbed person if that is like his father. A father who rejects his daughter teaches her to be afraid of men because of her emotional pain related to being rejected. She will long for a father's love throughout her lifetime and will unconsciously select men who are not Loving with whom to have meaningful interpersonal relationships. The daughter will believe that she is not worthy of being Loved by a man and will tend to attract to herself men who are immature and emotionally needy. The pattern of being involved with the "wrong" men continues until she recovers psychologically from the rejection. Usually, recovery requires professional help.

A common example of a family system that harms the son emotionally is Edward. I am helping Edward who is in a recovery process. Edward was born into a family in which his mother was the dominant person. He was the first born of two children, one son and one daughter. The dynamics within the family were that Edward's mother became overly invested in her son from birth on while his father was relegated to a very unimportant role in his son's life. This pattern continued throughout Edward's development as a child, teenager and adult.

The net result of Edward being overly involved emotionally with his mother and under involved emotionally with his father is that he failed to grow psychologically. What I mean is that Edward did not develop into an emotionally mature person. Instead, he lives life as a child even though he appears to others to be a fully functioning man. He deceives people into thinking that he is a man psychologically because he is a man physically. Edward does not show his childish thoughts, attitudes and orientation to life to others. On the surface, he behaves like a typical man.

He is married, has children, works hard to make a living, talks to neighbors, has sex with his wife, has relationships with family members, etc. However, what we see on the outside is not what is happening on the inside. The inner person is very much a child who "needs his mommy."

Edward goes through life feeling very anxious and depressed. His life is ruled by his obsessive-compulsive behavior which helps him to cope on an everyday basis. In fact, his capacity to love is severely restricted because his emotional life centers around his dependency on his mother to attend to him, value him and adore him. He is fixated on being a "good boy" of whom his mother would be proud.

What do we know about the inner workings of a person like Edward? Inside are intense negative emotions that are hidden behind an elaborate defense structure. These emotions include fear, anger and rage, shame, loneliness and pain. Edward feels inadequate as a man and tries constantly to prove his "manliness." He confuses his need for a mother with his desire to have a significant relationship with a woman. He questions constantly his identity as a male because he feels weak and powerless and unable to assert himself when necessary.

Edward has made his mother the role model instead of his father. As a child, Edward could only have superficial relationships with other children and so he spent much time by himself in his own world of fantasy and dreams. He is a "lost soul" who hides from others because he anticipates rejection and disapproval once he is discovered to be a frightened child and not a highly successful man.

Another example of a family system that is harmful to the children is when the father is the dominant parent and the mother is passive and submissive. What we prefer to see in families is that the parents work as a team sharing the power between them equally. They take turns being in charge of the children and they work collaboratively to establish family rules. Neither parent assumes the top-dog position or the under-dog position because they respect each other's authority as a parent. When they do not agree, they try to talk it out or they find a way to compromise. The children see their parents as co-managers of the family team.

In a family in which the father is "lord and master" the children will suffer psychologically. It may not look like it to outside observers but the children will have issues which are serious in nature. An example is Patricia who is a client that is doing psychological work on herself.

She is the oldest child in a family of three children. Instantly, she became "daddy's little girl" after her birth. She will remain in that role throughout her lifetime because it is a trap that feels good to both she and her father. Her father needs her to be that "special" person in his life and she became addicted to being so important to her father. Trapped in this role retarded seriously her psychological growth. Patricia became so focused upon pleasing her father and being so important to him emotionally by living up to his expectations for her that she was unable to develop a positive sense of self and positive self-regard.

A further problem for Patricia was that being her father's favorite in the family caused conflict between Patricia and her mother and her siblings. Patricia's relationship with her mother became strained because of how important she was in her father's emotional world. For the emotional well-being of the family, we want the mother and not the daughter to be the single most important person in the father's emotional world. Otherwise, an imbalance within the family will develop. In Patricia's case, both of her siblings were envious and angry about her relationship with her father. They rejected Patricia and treated her with disdain. Her mother, feeling hurt emotionally because her husband "loved" Patricia more than her, distanced herself from Patricia physically and emotionally. Losing her mother's involvement was very damaging psychologically to Patricia. She did not have her mother's Love, emotional support and assistance that are so valuable to a girl who is growing up to be a woman.

In summary, I would like to say that every child born on planet Earth needs Love from both parents, if at all possible, no matter what that child brings in with him or her. I believe that every person comes to the earthly experience as a spiritual being who is then provided a human body so that he or she can live, learn and succeed on the physical plane. Receiving Love from parents gives that individual a very good start in life. Conversely, none or very little Love from parents not only handicaps that person but puts him or her in jeopardy for a life that may lead to criminal behavior, a pattern of negative interpersonal relationships, failure at school, home or on the job, drug and alcohol addiction, serious emotional problems such as depression, anxiety disorders and obsessive-compulsive disorders, a feeling of being lost and a pervasive feeling of sadness and helplessness. The bad news is that parental Love deprivation is harmful and emotionally crippling. The

GOOD news is that there is a process of recovery available that really works?

5

THE RECOVERY PROCESS

If we are fortunate enough to be born to Loving parents, then we set out on our journey with maximum emotional support. They are models of Love and so our parents are instrumental in teaching us how to evolve into self-Loving individuals.

Loving parents willingly accept responsibility for their actions. They take the role of being a parent very seriously and so they learn valuable parenting skills to use as their children develop mentally, physically, emotionally and spiritually. Loving parents take an active interest in their children's lives and wholeheartedly make the sacrifices that need to be made for the well-being of their kids. Their level of involvement is high and they approach their children

56

with a selfless attitude. They support and encourage their children to discover their true selves which include learning about their strengths and weaknesses. Loving parents sponsor their children to become independent thinkers so that they can form their own opinions about life on planet Earth. Furthermore, they teach their sons and daughters about personal growth by being growth oriented themselves. Loving parents know the importance of their children developing into psychologically fit, spiritually minded and emotionally mature adults. They show by example the necessity of working hard on self-improvement throughout one's lifetime.

On the other hand, unloving parents hinder their children's growth which makes the child's journey that much harder. These children are less likely to be on a path of personal growth. Consequently, the children are not fit psychologically and will not evolve into psychologically fit individuals without participating in an effective process of recovery.

When I refer to unloving parents, I do not mean that all unloving parents are evil minded. Evil, by my definition, is the intention to do harm. I believe that it is true that there are some parents that want to take their anger and hatred out on their children. The children become scapegoats and their parents feel satisfied when they see their children suffering emotionally and physically.

The non-evil minded unloving parents cannot help themselves because they have failed to thrive emotionally during their lifetimes. Often, they work hard as parents but fail to provide their children with the positive emotional supplies that they need. LOVE does not flow from these parents and so their children are deprived. Deprived children are psychologically abused children which means that they have severe emotional pain within which is probably blocked and converted into self-hatred, negative behavior which may be directed externally at home, at school or towards peers and authority figures. LOVE deprived children are depressed whether it shows or not. Many children have the ability to cover up the depression behind a smiling face or a fun-loving attitude. Often, they have friends and live normal looking lives. Their parents, teachers, other relatives and involved adults do not know how much these children are suffering inside.

Years can go by and no one knows that these children are seriously depressed.

Sometimes, the depression shows itself only when these children become adults.

As far as they know, they are "fine" psychologically. It is their belief that they do not need professional help. What happens is that they go about their lives until something happens which brings the underlying depression to the surface. Usually, a crisis develops which is impossible to ignore and to avoid. Common examples are severe financial problems, marital difficulties, health issues, loss of a job, death of a parent, spouse or trusted friend, physical injury and legal problems.

Typically, the person in crisis begins to feel depressed but believes that it will pass quickly. The person tries to make him or herself "feel better" by buying things, going places, talking to friends and starting new projects. When the depression does not go away and, in fact, gets worse, the person does one of two things which are to make an appointment with the family doctor to obtain a prescription for medication or try self-medication by purchasing remedies that are sold over-the-counter in drug stores or health food stores. It is easier for most people to take pills when depressed than to consult with a mental health professional.

It has been my experience that most family practitioners will prescribe anti-depression medication without ever recommending a mental health professional to their patients. I believe that family doctors mean well and are motivated to relieve patient symptoms as quickly as possible. The doctors have been approached by representatives of the pharmaceutical companies who have touted their drugs and have given the doctors many samples. The doctors have not been trained adequately to understand that anti-depression medication MAY relieve symptoms but relieving symptoms only serves to cover up the underlying depression that has been there for many, many years.

It is important to keep in mind that medical doctors are trained to think of depression as an illness rather than a sign of underlying emotional disturbance. Depression can be thought of as a wake-up call to the depressed person that something is seriously wrong in the psychological domain. What I mean is that a depressed person is telling us that he or she is feeling self-hatred, intense anger which may or may not be conscious, feelings of helplessness and powerlessness and interpersonal loneliness and alienation. Instead of just providing medication to the depressed person, why do we not reach out to the person and offer a program that will provide the individual with Love and the opportunity to experience and release inner emotional pain and anger? In addition, the person will learn how to develop an attitude of self-empowerment, become able to form close and intimate interpersonal relationships, learn how to prevent becoming involved with toxic and abusive people and to find the path that will promote growth psychologically, mentally and spiritually.

The program that I have just described exists and can be made available to those that are interested. The program is provided by trained helpers who are familiar with all of its elements. I will refer to the program as the Recovery Process or RP as I describe it in more detail.

People who need a RP should be thought of as emotionally traumatized individuals even though, on the surface, they may appear to be fine. We all rely on wearing masks in public and so we are fooled into thinking that a RP program is not needed. We do not have to be on the verge of an emotional and/or physical collapse to need a RP. It is not unusual for emotionally traumatized people to function normally in society. Most people believe that emotionally traumatized people look emotionally traumatized as they present themselves in public. REALLY NOT THE CASE! We are taught, as children, to hide our emotional pain, insecurities, fears and emotional traumas from others if at all possible. It becomes second nature for us to put a smile on our face, talk optimistically about the future and to appear self-confident and at ease interpersonally. It is as though we take all of our emotional pains, insecurities, fears and emotional traumas and hide them in an internal storage locker which is behind a very sturdy wall. On some deeper level within us we have no intention of opening that storage locker and we will resist anyone who wants to get behind our sturdy wall. However, recovering from emotional trauma which is a psychological healing process requires that we take down our wall, expose our storage locker to others and participate in a program that is comprehensive and holistic in nature. What I mean is that the program focuses on the well-being of our physical, mental, emotional and spiritual selves.

The RP requires that participants have individual and group sessions throughout its duration. Every participant needs hours of one to one time with that special staff person that has been chosen for him or her by the program director. It is imperative that the participant and staff member be matched in such a way that they can work together effectively and successfully. The participant will need considerable emotional support in order to access and then resolve the core issues that exist.

Group participation is a necessity for anyone working the RP. Each participant will need to attend weekly, monthly and quarterly groups and will remain in the same groups so that continuity can take place. Much of the actual work of breaking down inner walls and opening the storage locker is done in the groups. There will be a highly trained and experienced staff member helping the participants in each group session. The plan is that discussing the issues and learning about the RP takes place within individual sessions and the experiential work is promoted within the groups.

There are many aspects of the RP that will be experienced by each participant. All of us are individuals that learn in our own specific way. Some of us are visual learners and some of us are auditory learners. Nevertheless, all participants will be provided with a program that promotes psychological and spiritual growth. The aspects that will be included are the workings of the mind (mental processes), our emotions, utilizing our intuition, the need for touching, the importance of having the friendship of others, being reached and, of course, the giving and receiving of LOVE.

6

OUR BELIEFS

We are all programmed during our growing up years, *MANY*
mainly by our parents and teachers, to have certain *FALSE*
beliefs. These beliefs are in our minds until the day that
we die. There is no way to erase them other than by
destroying parts of the brain. It is important to keep in
mind that almost everyone on planet Earth has a belief
system that influences that person's behavior,
emotional reactions and moods. Our mind analyzes data
coming in from the senses and then "thinks" about the
information before deciding what to do. The role of the
belief system is to help us to understand the data as to
whether or not the information is meaningful or should
be ignored. Our beliefs are considered truths by each
person and, therefore, considered to be very valuable
and necessary for survival.

The problem is what do we do about beliefs that are nonsensical and erroneous? Examples are "I deserve to suffer emotionally throughout my lifetime," "I am not worthy of Love," "I should be ashamed of myself," "I will never prosper emotionally and financially," "I am powerless to change my life so that I become a happier and more successful person," "I must wall myself off from others in order to protect myself," and "I cannot ever recover from the emotional traumas of the past."

I wish that we would have the ability to erase these negative beliefs from our mind but we do not. What we can do is to create a new set of beliefs that will compete with the old beliefs so that one day the new beliefs will replace the old ones. By this is meant that we live our lives guided by the new beliefs rather than the old set of beliefs.

It takes a long time and a lot of work to shift from a negative thinking pattern to a positive one. After all, people who are in the RP have had their belief systems operational for many, many years. It is human nature for people, in general, even those in recovery, to cling to the old beliefs in order to feel more secure. Most people feel some anxiety when asked to give up the familiar for something new. That is why continuous emotional support is needed for everyone who is willing to experience RP.

Recovering from emotional trauma requires each and every person to become more aware (conscious) of their thought patterns so that constructive work and improvement can take place. Very often, a person will not know what he or she is thinking that is causing emotional distress. I subscribe to the theory that it is our thoughts that cause us to react emotionally to situations rather than the situations themselves. An example is that someone you value rejects you and you feel emotional pain or what is referred to as hurt feelings. We have been programmed to think that the rejection itself has caused the pain when it's really our thoughts about the rejection that cause the pain. Let me explain further. I create within myself a hurt feeling about the rejection because I am thinking that I need emotional support from the person and not rejection. I feel sad that I have been rejected by someone who means so much to me. If I did not feel needy of the rejecting person's emotional support then I would not feel pain when I was rejected.

The problem is that, often, we do not know what we are thinking before we react emotionally to other people or to certain events. With the professional assistance we would receive in the RP it would be possible to learn about our unconscious thought patterns and what to do about them.

In summary, the thought that someone has hurt our feelings by yelling and criticizing us is untrue. Feelings arise in the brain. Therefore, no one can ""hurt" our feelings unless that person attacks our brain with a bullet or some other device. We need to take responsibility for all of our emotional reactions rather than blame others for why we get emotionally upset. By taking ownership of our thought patterns and the created emotional reactions we can do work on ourselves so that the quality of life improves.

Our mind is very much like a computer in that it takes in data, analyzes it and then provides a response. We have senses that provide the brain with information about the external world in order to help us survive in life. We are taught by parents and others about the dangers that threaten our well-being. Learning about these threats gives us the opportunity to protect ourselves as well as we can. We learn as children not to touch hot objects or we will get burned. We learn not to play with sharp things or we might get cut. We learn not to run into the street without looking first or we could get hit by a car. There are many other examples of things to be learned by children for their self-protection. Our computer mind analyzes data based upon the programming mainly by our parents. Their way of analyzing data becomes our way of analyzing data throughout our lifetime. What our parents considered dangerous and threatening is stored in our minds without exception. Once learned, it cannot be unlearned. If we are taught by our parents that criticism from others is something to be ashamed of then we will always have a reason to avoid it. Becoming an approval seeker is one way to minimize disapproval and criticism from others. Taking the time to understand the ways that we have been programmed is highly beneficial. We need to know what is in our programming so that we can decide for ourselves what is truly dangerous and threatening and not just be clones of our parents.

Emotionally traumatized people have learned that their parents are dangerous individuals who they cannot fully trust. Physical and/or psychological trauma experienced by children teaches them that the world is not a safe place. This belief remains locked in the mind of every child that has been traumatized. They develop ways to protect themselves from more trauma. Being interpersonally distant is a common way for children and then as grown ups to avoid risking more trauma from others. People trying to avoid more trauma tend to be superficial in their relationships, fantasy oriented, out of touch with their emotions, addicted to substances, compulsive in their behavior, have problems with depression and anxiety and try to appear normal in public. They concentrate on not looking traumatized. They are in hiding from the world.

Being a psychologist working with emotionally traumatized people for so many years has been a privilege for me. I consider myself blessed that so many psychologically injured individuals have trusted me enough to show me their emotional wounds and scars. It takes great courage to allow a complete stranger in the sanctuary of their mind. I have learned so much about the human mind from emotionally traumatized persons who were intent on healing themselves. They gave me the opportunity to participate in their healing, which I consider an honor and to learn about the RP.

7

OUR EMOTIONAL SELVES

Every human being has an emotional self that is built in and stays active throughout their lifetime. We are not just thinkers but also we are emotional reactors to both internal and external events. Some people try very hard to ignore their emotions but they are there anyway. It has to do with early childhood experiences and how the parents or other care givers respond to the baby. For example, newborns cannot talk to us and tell us what they need. They have to communicate using their emotions of joy, anger and pain by being in a happy mood, screaming or crying. It comes naturally to infants to be highly charged at times during the day. Different parents react differently to the emotions of their child. There are parents that are comfortable dealing with the baby's feelings and there are parents that are not. We can see that parental reactions will have a lot to do with the development of the emotional self of the child.

A common example is a strong willed child who wants to be picked up and cuddled by his or her parent. If ignored, the baby begins to cry and then screams in order to get what it wants. If that baby is yelled at by the parent who does not want to be bothered and the negative interaction between parent and child is repeated often, eventually the child learns to stop communicating its feelings and withdraws more and more inside itself. Over time, the baby learns to keep quiet rather than asserting its emotional needs.

For a non-strong willed child, having its feelings ignored is very discouraging and there is even a greater likelihood of emotional withdrawal. The withdrawn child becomes used to feeling alone and isolated. The parents may not know that their child is now lost emotionally. Instead, they may believe falsely that the child is doing well psychologically because it hardly ever creates a fuss.

It is so important to a child's growth mentally, emotionally and spiritually that his or her positive and negative feelings be acknowledged by the parents and the parents encourage the child to express feelings openly and honestly. Otherwise, the child's natural tendency to numb out takes over. Once significantly numbed out, it is very hard to reverse the process. It takes a lot of work for a numbed out person to start feeling again. The good news is that it will happen if the person participates in RP.

What happens to negative feelings that are no longer felt and communicated by the child?

I believe that they are stored in the mind indefinitely unless something internal or external triggers them. Once triggered, the child, adolescent or adult now knows that the feelings exist.

The choice for the person is to keep these feeling private or start sharing them with others. My hope is that such an individual, faced with this difficult decision, will seek out Loving attention from appropriate relatives, friends and/or professionals.

It is now time to discuss the intense negative emotions that need to be processed by an emotionally traumatized mental health consumer. The negative emotions are contained within the emotional self and their names are anger, sadness and fear. Being able to process these feelings successfully requires that the consumer participate in a program that provides continual emotional support from others and receives the individual and group experiences that are needed. It cannot be done if the services provided by the mental health professional include only one to one attention. Though some processing of emotions can take place, consumers will not be able to bring into awareness the intense anger (rage), psychological pain and terror that have been covered up for years unless more than one to one attention is given.

It has been my experience that the majority of mental health providers do not feel comfortable in a process that exposes the intense negative feelings carried around by their clients. It may come as a surprise to most readers to learn that most mental health professionals are not required to work through their own intense negative emotions which are blocked and that they have not been trained to help others to do it. What happens, typically, is that it is the mental self rather than the emotional self of the client that is given most of the attention. Generally speaking, the emotional self is ignored in sessions and even discouraged from showing itself. The erroneous belief held by many mental health professionals is that emotionally traumatized individuals will recover satisfactorily if their thoughts and not their feelings are addressed. The effective healing of psychological wounds can take place only if the blocked negative emotions of consumers are brought to consciousness.

Having an emotional self is a gift from the Universe because it adds a richness to our lives that would not be there if humans could only think and not feel. The problem is that many, many children are not programmed properly by their parents with regards to having positive and negative emotions. For example, many fathers teach their sons not to honor sad feelings and that crying is to be avoided at all costs. The message is that boys who cry are "sissies." At the same time, there is a tendency for mothers to teach their daughters that feeling angry is to be avoided or a label of "bitch" may be applied. The rule of thumb for most parents seems to be that sons are allowed to be angry and girls are allowed to be sad and to feel hurt emotionally. Both groups of children are taught not to feel fear and terror. The programming that I just described causes children to be in conflict with their emotional selves. Instead of "owning" their emotions, youngsters become alienated from their feelings which adversely affects growth in the mental and spiritual selves.

All children, adolescents and adults need to know that all emotions are acceptable to have as we live our lives from birth to death. It is important to take responsibility for having an emotional self even though we may feel uncomfortable with some or all of it. This is the case especially for the emotionally traumatized person because of the tendency to hide the emotional self from public view. Why is this tendency there? A child who lives without Love does not feel safe and secure. Instead, the child feels helpless, vulnerable and at the mercy of others. For self-preservation reasons, the child goes into hiding by withdrawing into a very private inner world.

Very often, the child uses disguises when interacting with others. The main disguise is when the individual presents himself or herself as a "happy and contented" person in society. It is not unusual for friends, relatives and significant others to be fooled by the disguise. Another commonly used disguise is becoming a successful achiever in one or more ways such as professionally, educationally, monetarily and occupationally and then walking around and showing a proud and worthwhile attitude. Little do we realize that behind the disguise is a person who feels worthless, unlovable, lost and self-hating.

Being emotionally traumatized does not preclude a person from becoming rich and famous. There are millions of people who are seriously wounded psychologically and do not know it. They live "normal" lives, functioning well on the job, earning a living, get married and have children, attend religious services, get along with their neighbors, hold public office, help others and much more. In spite of the wounds, they turn out to be well-intentioned and responsible people. How would we know that they are emotionally traumatized? There are signs such as taking anti-depressant and anti-anxiety medication, needing to take sleeping pills regularly and having chronic physical stress-related symptoms such as headaches, low back pain, high blood pressure, frequent illnesses, digestion difficulties and skin disorders to name a few. There are other telltale signs such as losing one's temper repeatedly, compulsive eating and drinking, chronic interpersonal relationship problems, treating others scornfully and meanly, settling for a long-term job that is not challenging and growth producing and having difficulty being Loving with family members and others.

For a person in RP, it is necessary to make a change from always depending on disguises to revealing the emotional self to those key people who are there to help. I am referring to the RP staff members, group mates, friends and relatives that can be trusted to be providers of Loving attention. Not an easy thing to do for a person who has and still does hide intense negative emotions from being exposed. Working hard so that these emotions come to the surface is an act of bravery. Over the years, I have witnessed many people dropping out of the recovery process rather than doing the required work. The courage is just not there! The need to avoid owning and then exposing their grief, rage and terror is too strong to overcome. I have no doubt that those who have dropped out have regrets and that they know that their impairments and associated symptoms will remain throughout the rest of their lives.

The good news is that it is never too early or too late for a person to do RP work. Dropouts can always come back and continue processing the emotional self. There are no age restrictions so that children, seniors and people in between can benefit. Every person has an emotional self and has the right to have the feelings that are there. Every person has the right to experience life as an emotional being whether or not parents and others approve.

Having feelings and expressing them do not necessarily go hand in hand. Cursing your boss may get you fired. Yelling at your parents may get you punished. Telling a friend about your angry feelings may cost you the relationship. Crying in public may lead to being ridiculed. Even though expressing positive and negative feelings is so important for our growth, we need to be aware that sometimes it is necessary for the individual to keep the emotional self hidden.

A safe place to express all emotions is a RP group. Intense negative feelings can be shared without bringing on undesirable consequences. Staff members are highly trained as facilitators and use techniques that work. Group mates provide the emotional support that is needed. Frequent group sessions weekly and monthly are required.

8

INTUITION

All human beings are blessed with a gift called intuition that is built in from birth. Other names for intuition are the "inner voice," the "higher self," the "inner knower" and a "gut feeling."

Our intuition serves as a guidance mechanism that keeps us on the right track as we go about our mission of becoming Loving people. It is there to help us master the lessons of being able to give and to receive Love.

Human brains contain two halves called the left and the right hemispheres. The left hemisphere provides us with the ability to think rationally and logically and the right hemisphere provides us with intuition. We can become confused when the logical mind tells us one thing and our intuition tells another. Which one do we listen to depends upon the programming that we received mainly from our parents.

My training as a psychologist emphasized the use of the left side of my brain as I endeavored to provide assistance to my clients. The professional books that I read focused on left brain oriented interventions. Being a new mental health worker, I felt somewhat overwhelmed with the responsibility of helping others and so I stuck with my training as much as possible. I tried to use my logical mind when dealing with emotionally traumatized individuals. IT DID NOT WORK WELL AT ALL. I became dissatisfied with the results and wondered about what else I could do. Gradually it dawned on me to allow my intuition to take over and that is what I did. My ability to be an effective helper improved dramatically.

I believe that a higher power exists and that it provides us with guidance throughout our lifetime.

It is my intuition that connects me with the higher power. My name for the higher power is the Universe while others prefer the names of God or Lord. No matter the name, the meaning is the same. There is a spiritual domain and we are spiritual beings living within that domain. As a spiritual being, I represent Love and Light and not darkness. Goodness exists as does evil and I need my intuition to keep me on the right path.

Intuition is an open channel for Universal guidance. I have come to believe that angels exist as helpers to all of us and that they Love us, watch over us, teach us and keep us company as we grow in all of the four domains. Believing in angelic guidance came later in my career and certainly was never mentioned during my years of training as a psychologist. The problem is that the open channel can become blocked and that the Universal guidance does not get through to our consciousness. When this happens, we feel lost, helpless and afraid.

I think of intuition like a radio channel that is giving us information all of the time. However, like a radio there can be interference, noise that blocks the radio's transmissions. I am referring to the presence of emotional distress as the cause of the interference.

When I was a young psychologist I relied heavily on using techniques that were developed by recognized experts in the field of mental health. It needs to be stated very definitely that there are many useful approaches and interventions that are truly beneficial to emotionally traumatized people. The problem that I have is that there is a tendency in the field to match an individual to the theoretical approach rather than matching the approach to the individual. Being able to match individuals and approaches successfully requires the use of intuition on the part of the mental health worker. There are literally hundreds of different theories and interventions that have been proposed to help promote psychological healing ranging from listening techniques to heavy-duty confrontation and using or not using psychiatric medications such as anti-depressants and tranquilizers. It is our intuition that will tell us what to do with a particular person based upon what is needed truly by that individual. The mental health professional's intuition will guide him or her to set up a program of healing if it is allowed to do so by that professional. Unfortunately, it has been my experience that the process does not work that way. Instead, the mental health provider gets into the habit of treating all the clients in much the same way because the professional is most comfortable with a particular intervention or theoretical approach. The idea is that Love is needed whether or not drugs or other interventions are used. The intuition of the mental health worker is trying to get that message through but the worker may not be listening.

As I stated before, we are blessed with a gift from the Universe called intuition. It is built in and not acquired. It is there so that we can have a successful journey. I have come to rely on my intuition almost exclusively as compared to relying on my logical mind as a helper and as a person. I have worked long and hard to keep the channel open. Universal guidance is provided via the channel and I am grateful for the information. What I have learned is that RP unblocks the channel of emotionally traumatized people so that they have now Universal guidance for themselves which increases a sense of empowerment and self-confidence. It takes a lot of work to open a blocked channel. The good news is that it can be done by everyone who does the right work.

Emotionally traumatized individuals are severely emotionally distressed even though the distress is hidden from others or even themselves. The presence of intense negative emotions interferes with the ability to receive intuitively based information. The person is so wounded and upset that he or she, beginning in early childhood, becomes highly dependent on his or her conscious mind in order to try to survive in a perceived hostile and scary world. Questions like "What am I going to do?", "Who will save me?", "How can I escape to a safe place?" and "Does anyone Love me?" keep the individual tied to the conscious mind as a security blanket. Staying fixed to the conscious mind may bring a feeling of comfort in that there is hope that answers can be found.

Using one's conscious mind shifts the person from the emotional self to the mental self which serves to distance the child or adult away from the negative emotions that are there.

The ability to use intuition comes back slowly for people in RP. Identifying and releasing intense negative emotions is necessary if the blocked channel is to open. Once there is at least partial unblocking, individuals are given instruction in accessing their intuition. They are now ready to shift their reliance from conscious mind to their intuition. Aiding the transition is being taught how to meditate and then being encouraged to meditate often. However, the use of meditation is discouraged in emotionally traumatized persons until core emotions are identified and released. Otherwise, there is a real possibility that the emotionally traumatized individual will choose to practice meditation which can have a calming effect as a way of avoiding doing difficult core work. I believe in the benefits of meditation. The only issue for me is when to promote its use in the RP.

The higher self serves as an internal guidance system in the same way that a map tells us where we are on planet Earth. Information is provided by the higher self so that we can experience maximum growth in all four domains. As a spiritual being, I am here to master the giving and receiving of Love and I need my inner voice to make it possible. I would not be able to have a successful journey without it.

Emotionally traumatized people need to heal themselves by doing relevant work and having Loving helpers in their lives. The last thing they need is to be victimized more. Sometimes it is easy to spot a potential victimizer and sometimes it is not. Emotional needs, left over from childhood, can take us over when we meet someone new that appears to be a Lover when really only a lover. Taking on a lover is not a good idea for an emotionally traumatized person because the lover is coming from a selfish place, using the victim, which results in more psychic pain to process. The higher self is there to provide a warning that only love and not Love is available.

Hopefully, the channel is open enough so that the message is received. The higher self will try very hard to communicate to you who can be or not be a Loving person in your life.

There are many people on planet Earth that are toxic to our well-being because of their inner "darkness." It is important that we know who they are even though they are masquerading in public as Lovers or profess to being "goodness" oriented beings. When intuition is working, we know who the phonies are and we avoid them as much as possible. The rose-colored glasses are off and in their place is crystal clear vision.

9

Touching

All human beings need physical affection as newborns in order to develop properly psychologically. The need for physical affection continues as children become older. Children feel helpless and powerless much of the time and so being held and hugged often provides reassurance that the child is safe and secure. Throughout our lifetime, being touched tenderly and warmly aids our growth into emotionally mature individuals.

Developing in the womb provides the fetus with continual touching by the membranes within the uterus. There is a sense of being connected to the mother which is a part of every fetus existence.

It is shocking and somewhat traumatic to be thrust out or be surgically removed from the womb. The sensations of being immersed in warm liquid, feeling physical contact with the mother and having all of your needs satisfied are very pleasurable. After birth, the newborn loses contact with mother for some amount of time and now feels a sense of isolation. Hopefully, the newborn is quickly in the arms of a Loving mother who touches her child with positive energy.

What happens if the child is not given Loving attention by the mother after the birth? Perhaps the mother is depressed and maintains psychological distance from her child. Perhaps she is unable physically to hold and give affection to the newborn. Perhaps she is an angry mother who did not want a baby of her own. The bonding process between mother and child is impaired which causes emotional trauma to the offspring. Such a child, and there are millions of them, will be seriously injured psychologically during their lifetime. They will need RP which promotes healing of the wound.

Trying to recover from a lack of maternal Loving attention which includes positive touching is a very hard thing to do. It is easier if that child received

Loving touching from someone else like the father, another relative or some Loving adult. However, the trauma does not go away just because another person was available. The mother-child connection is vitally important to the child's emotional well-being. Some kind of impairment within the child will occur if maternal Love and touching are not provided. Certainly, the child's psychological growth will be stunted. By this is meant that the child will remain emotionally immature throughout his or her lifetime basically being a little girl or a little boy who has never grown up.

Emotionally traumatized individuals need to be touched in a Loving way throughout their process of recovery. It is not enough to just talk to them, listen to them and to provide them with a variety of group experiences. Recovering people need to be held often by others, males and females, who can provide Loving attention. The Loving touching helps the receiver to access the negative emotions that need to be felt and released. Being able to bring intense emotional pain into consciousness does not come easily. Receiving physical affection reassures the recipient that he or she is not going through this difficult ordeal alone. It is an act of bravery to delve into one's hidden negative emotions in order to feel them, make sense of them and share them with others.

Positive touching promotes positive connections between people. Hugging each other is a wonderful way for us to communicate that we care. We all need to know that we have come to planet Earth in order to grow physically, emotionally, mentally and spiritually and that Loving attention and Loving touching are essential if our growth is to take place. Without them, we fail to thrive in all spheres. Without them, children become impaired adults or even die prematurely. Without them, children live in a world that feels threatening and dangerous. Without them, children and adults live isolated lives with an underlying depressed mood. Without them, Life is hardly worth living. Yes

An important issue to discuss involves the training of mental health professionals with regards to touching their clients. The accepted rule of thumb in the field of mental health practitioners is DO NOT TOUCH YOUR CLIENTS AT ALL. This means especially do not hug clients and do not hold clients at all. Mental health practitioners include psychologists, psychiatrists, clinical social workers, mental health counselors and family therapists. The concern is that touching a client may be interpreted by the client as an act of seduction by the professional who wants to have a sexual and/or romantic relationship with the client. Loving touching is out. Not touching a client is considered to be a significant factor in that mental health practitioner's risk management program. In other words, the practitioner is fearful of being sued by the client if touching is involved.

Despite the warning of *DO NOT TOUCH CLIENTS*, many mental health professionals, including myself, do at times touch their clients. Some clients do not want to be touched under any conditions and should not be touched at all. For many other clients, they want some form of Loving touching from the professional involved during their RP work.

It is important to keep in mind that anyone needing the services of a mental health worker is emotionally traumatized whether or not it is called a CHEMICAL IMBALANCE. These people are carrying around significant emotional pain from early childhood experiences. Emotionally traumatized clients require

Loving attention especially from the professional that was chosen by the client to be a part of the healing process. Consumers of mental health services need to receive as much Love as possible especially from the practitioner who is being trusted to be a part of RP.

I know that even though Loving touching is therapeutic to people who are emotionally traumatized; many mental health professionals will shy away from it. Their training emphasized KEEP YOUR HANDS TO YOURSELF. I believe that Loving mental health professionals will know when to touch their clients and when not to touch their clients. I am confident that a Loving mental health worker has nothing to fear if Loving touching is used.

10

FRIENDS

Loving friends are essential to those individuals who are on a path of growth. Being able to grow from an immature child to a mature adult is a challenging process. There are many hurdles to overcome along the way and many limitations that have to be faced. We need friendship from the Loving people in our lives to insure a successful journey.

The most important people around us from the day we are born that can offer friendship are our parents. As I stated before, we come into life giving up the security and comfort of the womb.

It is a shock to the newborn baby that he or she has a brand new environment to experience. It requires a major adjustment on the part of the child. Parents who provide friendship to their offspring help greatly to aid the adjustment process.

I think that it is an unusual idea for most parents to be told that their newborn baby needs their friendship, and not just their care. What would a parent look like who is prepared to be a friend to the baby? The mother and/or father would feel joyful that their son or daughter is here.

We would see smiles on their faces and a desire to hug and kiss the newborn. There would be affection given and the parents would communicate a message of WELCOME into our lives.

The friendly parents would look forward to holding the baby tenderly and warmly. They would show an interested attitude and want to be involved in the caring for their child. Receiving friendship from his or her parents gives the newborn a wonderful start in life. Conversely, not receiving parental friendship handicaps the child right at the beginning of a new life on planet Earth.

To me, a friendship between two people means that they have committed themselves to the relationship. The length of time is not an issue. A friend wants to be in your life until that life ends. Each friend cares unconditionally for each other. Each one Loves the other.

By my definition, a friend provides Love, tolerance, emotional support, involvement, assistance, interest and a willingness to be a partner throughout life. Do friendships like this exist? They most certainly do!

I have been fortunate enough to have friendship given to me by many different people. I treasure my friends because I know how valuable they are to my well-being. Friends can be trusted with our secrets, fears, traumas, hopes and dreams plus so much more.

EVERY PERSON WHO SEEKS HELP FROM A MENTAL HEALTH PROFESSIONAL DESERVES AND NEEDS FRIENDSHIP FROM THAT PROFESSIONAL. It is crucial for an emotionally traumatized person who wants to heal to have the opportunity to establish a friendship with the mental health professional that is most involved. Of course, the client has the choice. Some emotionally traumatized persons will not in the short term or the long term choose to build a friendship with the mental health worker. If it does not happen, then progress in RP will be limited.

I know that recommending that a client and mental health professional build a friendship feels threatening to clients and professionals alike. My recommendation is based upon years of being involved in people's RP and not my training in graduate school. I am convinced that a friendship between a Loving mental health professional and a client is highly therapeutic. I am not recommending it to professionals who are not LOVING individuals.

I feel badly for any client who is receiving services from a mental health professional who is not a Loving individual. It confirms in the mind of the consumer that he or she is not Lovable. Nothing could be farther from the truth. ALL HUMAN BEINGS ARE WORTHY OF LOVE AND DESERVE IT NO MATTER WHAT THEY HAVE DONE IN THE PAST. Being unworthy of Love is a belief that many people have in their minds. People who are ashamed of themselves, especially those with emotional trauma, are convinced that no Love will ever come into their lives. I often hear the question "If my own mother and father did not Love me, how could anyone else?" My response is to make the point that having parents who are not Loving is not the fault of the offspring but rather signifies impairment in the parents.

Mental health consumers are coming to mental health professionals for Love when services are sought. Most consumers cannot admit to themselves or anyone else that Love is what they need. They crave a Loving friend to help them because there is so much pain and suffering within. Of course, it is covered up by the client who does not give himself or herself permission to ask for it. Instead, the consumer asks for other things such as medication, specific types of therapy, psychological insight or solutions to a myriad of problems. It is the responsibility of the mental health professional to know the REAL reason for the appointment and then help each consumer to face the truth and be able to get the Love that is needed.

Mental health professionals who are not Loving people are very comfortable providing the things stated above and not providing Loving friendship. They would argue that it is unprofessional to give clients Loving attention. These professionals are short changing their clients when they provide all other services minus the Love.

I am interested in empowering mental health consumers to ask for Love and friendship from the providers of mental health services. I encourage all emotionally traumatized clients to self-validate their need for Love and friendship if they intend to heal. It is clear to me that medication and therapy are not enough.

11

BEING REACHED

Built into every human being is the desire to be Loved by at least one significant person. Typically, it is the mother who is the first person that has the opportunity to provide the needed Love with the father being the second. Being a Loving parent creates a special connection between parent and child which promotes continual growth in all areas as the child develops. A Loved child is able to live in the world of "here and now." The child communicates his or her feelings easily and comfortably. It is obvious that the child is bonded to one or both parents because the baby looks contented and happy and appears to be thriving.

On the other hand, a Love starved infant stands out because it appears distant and removed. The process of withdrawing from the world has started because the child without Love feels insecure, discontented and rejected. The baby's world feels cold and empty and a life of feeling lost and isolated takes over. Hopefully, one day someone will come along who will try to reach and connect with that lost individual.

Children deprived of Love grow up into impaired individuals who have severe problems Loving others. They can be very active lovers who are convinced that there is nothing wrong with them psychologically. There is a story of a man that I met nearly forty years ago that illustrates the point that I am trying to make. Many years ago, I worked for a psychologist in Philadelphia. His clients who came to the office were given a battery of psychological tests which I administered. My job was to interpret the test results to each client so that every person would be informed about his/her emotional issues that needed work. I will never forget one man who came to get his test results but believed fully that he had no emotional problems whatsoever. Why did he come to my employer's office? His marriage was falling apart and he agreed to attend sessions with a psychologist in order to please his wife. He took the tests but was obviously skeptical and disinterested in getting feedback. It was as though he was doing me a favor when he came in to see me. I had given test results to many people prior to meeting with this man. Some were more defensive than others but all were able to be reached even minimally. By this I mean that all were able to acknowledge that there were at least some problems to work on even if they did not really understand where they come from, how to work on them, or the true nature and depth of the emotional issues involved. All but this one man who nearly laughed in my face when I told him, that he was in severe emotional pain, and did not know it.

It is hard to believe that a person could be suffering so much inside and have no realization at all. I learned much from this man early in my career. I had not really understood the nature of psychological defensiveness until I tried unsuccessfully to reach this man who felt so emotionally wounded deep within himself. More than thirty-five years ago I spoke to him of peeling the layers of the proverbial onion so that core issues could be uncovered. He asked me why a person would do such a thing. I answered that working out core issues would lead to psychological growth.

He asked me to tell him how he would feel if he uncovered emotional pain just supposing that it was there. I told him that he would cry and feel very sad, scared, vulnerable and needy of emotional support. He thanked me for the information, said that he did not think there was pain to uncover, and if there was he had no intention of digging it up. He said that he liked himself and except for a few marital problems, he did not need to look inside himself for covered up pain which he does not believe exists. I think that he stopped sessions with the psychologist shortly thereafter. Needless to say, I have had many repeat experiences with other people about inner pain over the years. Many with children and adolescents, as well as adults. Some people have a strong need to believe that they have no emotional pain inside and not just that it may be blocked or numbed out.

I do not know what happened to that man so many years ago. I doubt that he changed his mind and agreed to do the core work that was needed.

What I have learned is that even though the vast majority of people choose to stay numbed out, I have met and worked with others who are willing to go inside and examine themselves to find core issues. These people, though initially apprehensive, allowed me to try and reach them in a more than superficial way. To do so requires a great deal of courage and persistence by the person wanting to be reached. It is so much easier to avoid being reached than it is to actively participate in the process.

Harder still is not running away from the Loving friend doing the reaching when that person gets closer and closer to making the connection. Emotionally traumatized people long for emotional intimacy, but fear the closeness because of feelings of vulnerability. The urge to run away gets stronger and often results in the breaking of the relationship by the client. Others, managing to hang on and overcoming their fear and desire to hide, allow themselves to be touched with Love even for just a few precious moments.

I am sad to have to say that mental health professionals, for the most part, do not try to reach the mental health consumers that seek their services. Being reached is the underlying need that an emotionally traumatized person has whether we are talking about children, adolescents or adults. Most people feel frightened when they become lost physically and/or psychologically. It is human nature to want to avoid the unknown. There is a comfortable feeling associated with doing things in the same old way as compared to trying out new and unfamiliar actions or approaches to life. What I am describing applies to mental health workers as well as mental health consumers. Providers and consumers are not educated to know the importance of being reached. Since it tends to be an unfamiliar concept, we can expect for both groups to resist its implementation into their lives. I am hoping that some mental health professionals will read about the importance of reaching their clients and possibly put it into practice.

Clients need to be informed that they deserve to be reached and that being reached plays a major role in their recovery. The healing process requires that every emotionally traumatized individual be reached so that Love can be given by the provider and taken in by the consumer.

12

LOVE

Much has been written about Love over the centuries by novelists, poets, philosophers, mental health professionals and countless others. It is hard to find agreement among these writers as to what Love is and what Love is not. All of the different definitions add confusion to the topic and so we are left to ourselves to choose the explanation that makes the most sense. I have chosen the one that best suits my personality and my belief system. I will share my thoughts about Love with the admission that I am a spiritually based individual who is comfortable with that orientation.

When I first started out as a mental health provider, I was not spiritually based. I did not know the difference between Love and love. I had no graduate school courses about Love and so my work with clients involved love issues and not Love issues. I spent many years as a practicing psychologist before I understood the differences between the two. As I grew older, I became more and more spiritually based and less dependent upon psychological theories in my approach to helping emotionally traumatized people. I believe in the healing power of Love and discuss it openly with those mental health consumers that are interested. I have tried to be careful over the years not to discuss Love with consumers who want only to talk about love problems in their lives. They are not ready to take ownership of their spiritual self. Instead, they deal with life only mentally, emotionally and physically. Having such a limited approach to life means, that their healing will be very limited, also. A sad situation for all involved.

My belief is that human beings have a soul and not just a body. It is our soul that makes it possible to Love. It is our brain that makes it possible to love. We say that "I love my new car," or "I love my new home," or "I love my new diamond ring." What I mean is that I feel excited (euphoric) and emotionally high about something. An emotional response is involved.

The emotional self has taken over! In order to feel Love, I have to be experiencing my spiritual self. I believe that Love is positive energy generated by the soul. It creates new energy and also serves as a mechanism for positive energy, provided by the Universe or if you prefer, God, to flow through to the souls of people.

Souls connect with each other forming Love bonds which last a lifetime unless a person deliberately breaks the bond. There is a way for a person to disconnect his or her soul from another soul if that decision is made. We do not have to stay soul bonded to someone for the rest of our lives if we want to be free of that connection. Sometimes, a soul connection is formed with a person and it feels relevant. However, at some future time the relationship changes and the bond needs to go. It is permissible to terminate the bond at any time. There is no reason to feel guilty. The other person may find it painful emotionally to have the connection severed but we have the choice to do so. A common example is two people meet each other and proceed to build a relationship. A Love bond forms over time and eventually they marry. They live together harmoniously until one of the spouses begins to abuse the other spouse. The abuse continues and gets worse. The abuser refuses to seek professional help and ultimately the husband and wife separate and a divorce takes place. The abused spouse decides that it is necessary to break the bond with the abuser once and for all.

Emotionally traumatized individuals require Love in order to heal. They need to feel the positive energy being given to them by Loving helpers. The positive energy provides strength to the weakened person so that healing work can be done. Mental health consumers are constantly being drained of their energy by working hard to cope with life on a daily basis. It takes all of their energy to handle their responsibilities. There is very little extra energy left over for healing work. Keeping the intense negative feelings hidden is another drain of their energy. It should not be a surprise that most emotionally traumatized people look for a quick fix from mental health providers. Taking pills is a lot easier than doing core work. Settling for brief therapy interventions is a lot easier than delving into the subconscious mind. We cannot expect consumers to choose to do psychological restoration work if we do not provide them with the positive energy that is needed. Taking in Love from providers, friends, relatives and group mates makes the difference between maximal healing and minimal healing.

People who are trying to heal themselves emotionally need to be touched physically with Love often and by more than just one person during RP. In my groups, group mates as well as myself give Love freely to all participants. No one who wants Love is denied. Holding Lovingly an emotionally traumatized person who is feeling and sharing emotional pain is a necessity for healing to take place. This is the time for the emotionally wounded individual to be reached, consoled and comforted. Giving Love to that person makes the statement that Love is available and deserved.

A second special time for a consumer in RP to be given Love is when that person has experienced and shared their feelings of rage. Many people experience guilt and shame after revealing hateful emotions. There is a tendency to withdraw into themselves because of feeling embarrassed and an expectation of being criticized. Being offered Love after rage is shared is a way to communicate that all emotions are permissible and that being very, very angry at parents and others does not make you a Bad person who should be punished.

Being Loved during RP helps emotionally traumatized people to uncover the terror that is hidden within the inner world. I have come to learn that the most difficult core emotion to bring into consciousness is intense fear (terror). It is avoided at all costs. Terror is usually the last intense negative emotion that is processed. It has been my experience that a significant number of people terminate RP rather than do terror work. Those that continue in RP and attempt to resolve terror feelings require lots and lots of Love.

As I have stated before, I have a belief that the main reason that we are here on planet Earth is to learn to give and receive Love. Some people need to work more on one of the lessons and others need to work on both. What I mean is that I have witnessed people who are Loving by nature and give Love to others without difficulty. They are wonderful givers but may be unwilling receivers.

On the other hand, there are many people who can take in Loving energy but have none to give.

Emotionally traumatized persons are examples. It is as though they are full of psychic holes so that positive energy goes in but drains out almost immediately. The givers wonder where did the Love go because the receiver continues to feel negative in spite of being attended to Lovingly. Until some healing has taken place, people in psychological recovery need transfusions of Love as often as possible. Eventually, the individual learns to Love himself or herself so that less Love is necessary from others.

The RP works because of the healing power of Love. Without Love, mental health consumers may get some temporary symptom relief from their sessions with mental health providers but their real core emotional problems will not improve.

What I want to see is that all mental health consumers are given the opportunity to heal themselves with help from mental health professionals. I am sad to think that there are individuals who know that they are emotionally wounded and need to heal or they know that something is wrong inside of them that needs fixing but they are not going to receive the required assistance. My sense of fairness demands that I advocate for the rights of the consumers to those individuals providing mental health services to please consider becoming Loving helpers if you are not already!

ABOUT THE AUTHOR

Dr. Marvin Fredman has been a practicing psychologist for over thirty years. He obtained his doctorate degree in psychology from Temple University located in Philadelphia, Pennsylvania. Dr. Fredman is the past president of the Mental Health Association of Broward County Florida.

He has worked successfully with children, teens and adults as individuals, couples and families. His specialty has been and still is helping the emotionally wounded to heal themselves as part of a recovery process that brings Loving attention into their lives. Dr. Fredman believes that real healing takes place only when Loving attention is provided to consumers of mental health services. The absence of Loving attention makes emotional healing impossible and prevents spiritual and psychological growth from occurring. Deep seated negative emotions can be accessed and released if Loving attention is available.

Dr. Fredman lives with his wife and son in south Florida. He can be contacted by email @ mfredmanphd@gmail.com